The Voice of Our Times...

The Kid from Hoboken
Struts His Stuff

2161

- notes continued from back cover

James, while well known for his trumpet playing with Benny Goodman, did not yet have a famous big band. His orchestra struggled through 1939 although Sinatra had opportunities to record with James. His one hit with the band, "All Or Nothing At All," was unfortunately not released for several years. In Nov. 1939 he was offered a much more lucrative contract to join Tommy Dorsey. While with Dorsey during 1939-42, Sinatra became famous. He was heard regularly on the radio with Dorsey, both as a solo singer and as a member of the Pied Pipers. Sinatra was on 16 hit records including "I'll Never Smile Again." He was particularly popular with teenager girls who were called "bobby soxers" and sometimes screamed and sighed during his performances.

Sinatra was almost 27 in 1942 when he went solo but his popularity with teenagers continued for a few more years. His opening at the Paramount Theater on Dec. 30, 1942 was a major event. In addition to his radio appearances (including on Your Hit Parade), stage shows and hit records, he began to appear in his first movies including Anchors Aweigh and Take Me Out To the Ball Game.

As the 1940s were coming to a close, Frank Sinatra's career stalled. His recording career was suffering as producer Mitch Miller at the Columbia label insisted that Sinatra record more novelties. He was getting too old to be a teen idol, his newer movies were not doing that well, and his marriage to Ava Gardner was tumultuous. During 1951-52, many thought of Sinatra as a has-been.

But everything changed in 1953. Frank Sinatra won an Academy Award for Best Supporting Actor for his acting in From Here To Eternity. He signed with the Capitol label where for the next seven years he was able to record whatever he wanted. Gone were the novelties and instead Sinatra sang the high-quality standards of the 1930s and '40s that he loved with orchestras arranged by Nelson Riddle, Billy May or Gordon Jenkins. His concept albums were big sellers and include such classics as In The Wee Small Hours, Frank Sinatra Sings For Only The Lonely, Swing Easy, Songs For Swingin' Lovers and Come Fly With Me. Among the many great songs recorded by Sinatra during the 1950s were "Chicago (That Toddling Town)" which he performed in the 1957 movie The Joker Is Wild, "I've Got The World On A String (first recorded by him in 1953), "Night And Day," "I've Got You Under My Skin" (both from 1956), "Witchcraft" (from 1957) and "The Lady Is A Tramp." The latter song, which he performed in Pal Joey and recorded in 1958, was in his repertoire for the following 20 years. Other hits included "Young At Heart," "Angel Eyes," "One For My Baby" and "High Hopes."

By the late 1950s, Frank Sinatra was very much in his prime. In addition to his recordings, his movies did well, he occasionally hosted television specials, and his Las Vegas shows with the "Rat Pack" (Dean Martin, Sammy Davis Jr. and sometimes Joey Bishop and Peter Lawford) became legendary.

Unlike most other singers of his generation, Sinatra weathered the 1960s pretty well. His large audience never deserted him and he continued his successes in his live shows, on TV, in films, and his recordings. In 1961 he founded the Reprise label and his albums continued at the same quality as his records of the previous decade. He collaborated on a few projects with Count Basie (Sinatra-Basie, It Might As Well Be Spring and Sinatra At The Sands), Antonio Carlos Jobim and Duke Ellington Sinatra recorded "The Summer Wind" in 1966 and had signature hits with "My Way" (which summed up aspects of his life) and "Strangers In The Night." It did not matter much that the Beatles had risen to prominence and that rock was taking over the entertainment business; Sinatra still prevailed.

While Frank Sinatra retired during 1971-73, he came back in 1974 and performed for another 20 years. One of his last great hits was "New York, New York." It was originally sung by Liza Minnelli in the movie of the same name but, once Sinatra recorded it in 1979, it was his song.

The singer finally retired in 1994, passing away on May 14, 1998 at the age of 82. More than 15 years after his death, Frank Sinatra's music is still very much with us, through his recordings, movies and the many singers who do their best to be influenced by his artistry.

Scott Yanow,
author of 11 books including The Jazz Singers,
The Great Jazz Guitarists, Swing, Jazz On Film
and Jazz On Record 1917-76

The Voice of Our Times

CONTENTS

ISBN 978-1-941536-61-9

Theme From
"New York, New York"

Music by John Kander
Words by Fred Ebb

6

My Way

English Words by Paul Anka
Original French Words by Gilles Thibault
Music by Jacques Revaux and Claude Francois

MMO 2161

8

Chicago
(That Toddlin' Town)

Words and Music by
Fred Fisher

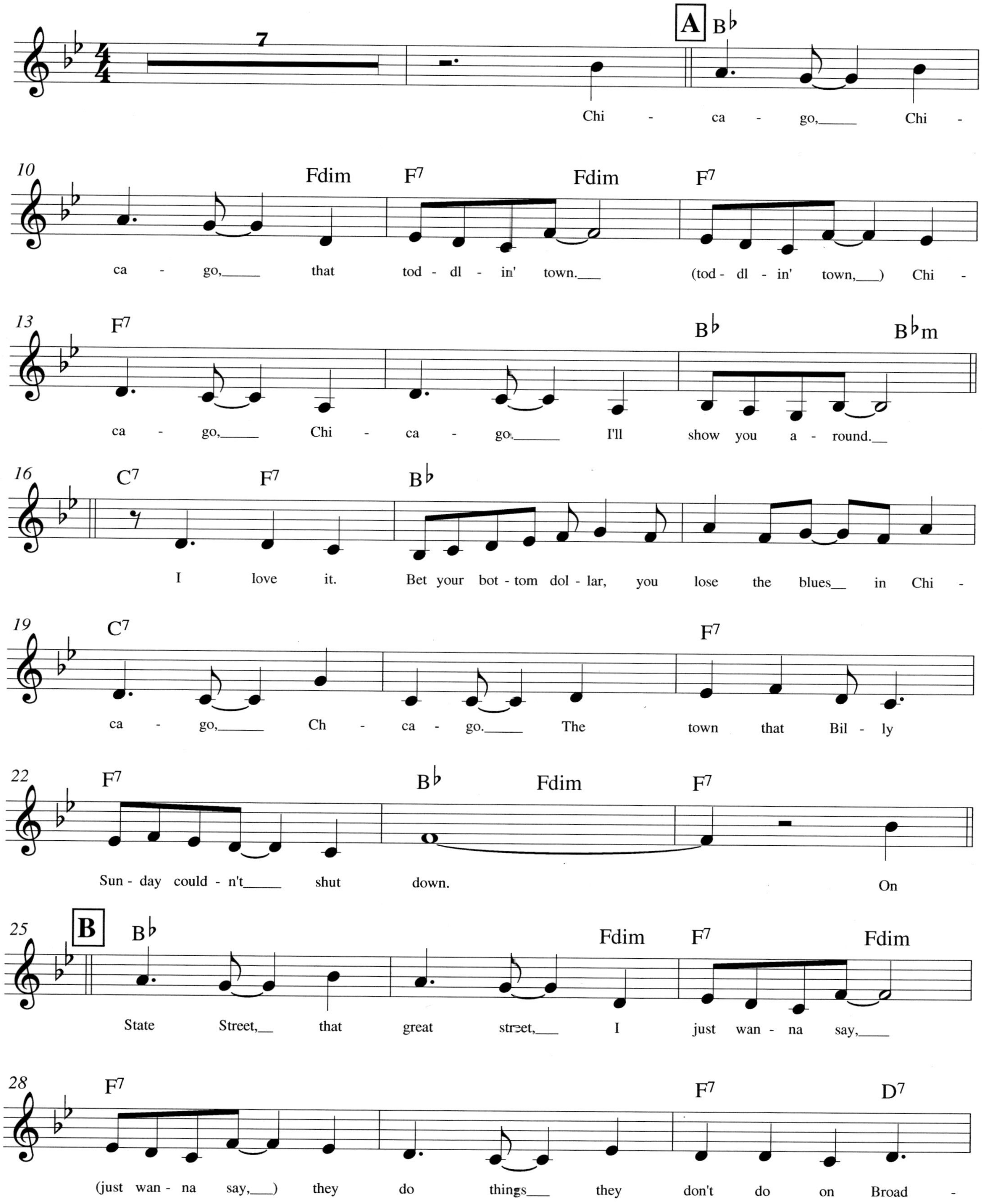

Strangers In The Night
adapted from A MAN COULD GET KILLED

Words by Charles Singleton and Eddie Snyder
Music by Bert Kaempfert

Witchcraft

Music by Cy Coleman
Lyrics by Carolyn Leigh

Summer Wind

English Words by Johnny Mercer
Original German Lyrics by Hans Bradtke
Music by Henry Mayer

I've Got The World On A String

Lyric by Ted Koehler
Music by Harold Arlen

Night And Day
from GAY DIVORCE

Words and Music by Cole Porter

22

MMO 2161

I've Got You Under My Skin

from BORN TO DANCE

Words and Music by Cole Porter

The Lady Is A Tramp
from BABES IN ARMS

Words by Lorenz Hart
Music by Richard Rodgers

MMO 2161

The Girl From Ipanema

Music by Antonio Carlos Jobim
English Words by Norman Gimbel
Original Words by Vinicius de Moraes

MMO 2161

All The Way

Words by Sammy Cahn
Music by James Van Heusen

MMO 2161

ISBN 978-1-941566-61-9